CONVERSATIONS WITH THE GOLF GOD

by

Robert K. Swisher Jr.

Text copyright © 2013 Robert K. Swisher Jr.

OPEN TALON PRESS

OTHER PUBLISHED NOVELS BY ROBERT K. SWISHER JR.
Historical Fiction: Trade and E-book
Published by Sunstone Press
The Land
Fatal Destiny

Contemporary Western Fiction: Trade and E-book
PUBLISHED BY SUNSTONE PRESS
How Far the Mountain
The Last Narrow Gauge Train Robbery
The Last Day in Paradise
Love Lies Bleeding
The Man From the Mountain

Literary: Out of Print
Published by Samisdat Press - Canada
American Love Story

Young Adult: Trade Only
Published by Echo Press California
The Weaver
Published by Sunstone Press
Only Magic

Humor: E-book and Trade
Conversations With the Golf God

Mystery Series: E-book and Trade
Bob Roosevelt Mystery Series – 4 novels

Contemporary Fiction: E-book only
Hope
A Circle Around Forever

Trade and E-book
Published by Open Talon Press
Vent
Grammar Nazis Are Not Always Rite, Right, Write
Vent Revisited
The Lonely Cowboy
How Bridge McCoy Learned to Say I Love you
Short stories and poetry in literary journals, articles in outdoor magazines.
Reviews by Publishers Weekly, Best Sellers, Library Journal, and many others.

**PUBLISHED BY
OPEN TALON PRESS**

**EDITORS: Sheila Awalt
COVER DESIGNER: Samantha Fury...Mike Nguyen
PRINT FORMAT: Samantha Fury
Images by andrewgenn@depositphotos.com
& Clker-Free-Vector-Images**

Part of this book is a work of fiction. For the fiction segments names, characters, places and incidents are either products of the author's imagination or are used fictitiously. Any resemblance to actual events, locales, or persons either living or dead, is entirely coincidental. Part of this work might be construed as non-fiction. If any of this book reminds you of yourself and you get offended by certain comments or remarks (corporations included since you are by law considered people) no harm, malice, libel, racism, discrimination, in any of the previous terms multitudes of forms and definitions, and any term that would come to mind by any other person, was intentionally intended either by me, my wife, my dog, my cat, my goldfish, my hanging plants, or any relative - this includes all and any life forms in the known and unknown universe that might share some of my DNA, and unknowingly, by either cosmic intervention, or a form of communication as yet unknown to mankind had anything to do with the writing of this book.

If you wish to use portions of this book for anything but reviews you must contact OPEN TALON PRESS or the author. Sorry, what can I say? We all know lawyers run the world. And to be honest we all know our politicians are controlled by big business interests who are also controlled by lawyers.

Library of Congress - In Publication Date

Swisher, Robert K, 1947 -
CONVERSATIONS WITH THE GOLF GOD A novel / by Robert K. Swisher Jr.
Summary: humor, golf, satire, lesson
ISBN is 978-0-9979096-9-2
LCN is 2021903823

DEDICATION

**FOR MY FATHER WHO TAUGHT ME
GOLF IS MORE THAN A GAME
BUT YOU HAD BETTER LAUGH AT IT**

THE GOLF GOD

TABLE OF CONTENTS

CHAPTER 1	THE GOLF GOD
CHAPTER 2	DOUBTING THOMAS
CHAPTER 3	A TRUE HISTORY OF THE GAME
CHAPTER 4	FREDDY
CHAPTER 5	THE SECRET TO PUTTING
CHAPTER 6	HOW TO MAKE A GOOD BET
CHAPTER 7	HEART AND THE PRIEST
CHAPTER 8	ALL THE QUESTIONS
CHAPTER 9	MONTANA
CHAPTER 10	GOLF TERMS
CHAPTER 11	THE GOLF GOD'S 14 RULES
CHAPTER 12	WHY WE PLAY GOLF

INTRODUCTION

This book is the true words of the Golf God which were dictated to me when he graced me with his not so spiritual presence. You may wonder why, since there are millions of golfers all over the world who are better players than I am, did the Golf God choose me to write his book? The Golf God chose me as his disciple for two reasons: I am broke and out of work, therefore I don't have any distractions, and, I am a lousy putter. A person who is a terrible putter must have great dedication to the game of golf to continue playing - either that or he is less intelligent than a rock.

The Golf God, in all his wisdom, has many purposes for this book. He wants to inform golfers of the true history of the game. He wishes golfers to know what common golf terms really mean. And, he is adamant that all golfers know his rules of golf - not the P.G.A. rules, which he finds amusing. He also told me to include in his book stories of real life golfers, stories about golf touring pros who complain that their game is off because they have to spend so much time counting their money or tuning up their helicopter are starting to bore him. He also desires to enlighten his followers to aspects of the game he feels have been neglected far too long, such as the fine art of making a good bet and how to correctly toss a golf club.

For choosing me as his disciple he allowed me to ask him a few questions about the game. I asked questions that are intended to lighten a golfer's burden and make the game easier. But the main reason he wanted me to write this book is he wants golfers to know he is real, and even though he is a god, he has never lost his human side. He needs us as much as we need him.

"Speed bump!"

AUTHORS NOTE:

The Fleece Muni is a real golf course and still a melting pot for thieves, hustlers, bankers, lawyers, a few drunks, and the working man. It is not a country club. The Priest, Heart, Montana, and Snake are real people (several of them are deceased - bless their larceny filled golfing souls.) The stories FREDDY, HEART AND THE PRIEST, MONTANA are true but for the benefit of the Golf God were slightly embellished for dramatic effect.

CHAPTER ONE
THE GOLF GOD

When man came upon the earth, whether it was God's will, space creatures planting members of their race on another planet, or an accidental mixture of sea water goo and electricity, it was unavoidable that one day man would begin to reason and with reason man began to ask questions. Questions, that no matter how educated man became, how mentally aware mankind grew, the questions remained unanswered? But, even unanswered, mankind cannot chase the questions from their minds. Remember the last good round of golf you ruined by starting to think too much?

Primitive man, unable to answer even the simplest questions offered stone fetishes to appease whatever force it was that kept making life difficult.

Besides starving most of the time and only normally living for twenty or thirty years he couldn't figure out why he couldn't hit a round rock off the ground with a stick and not hit it straight.

Since the stone fetishes mankind has invented a series of gods to try and answer all of our questions: Why are we here? Why do I think? Why is my kid a bum? Why does it always rain on Sunday just before my T-time? Why can't I make a three-foot putt to save my soul? Why do I keep moving my head and hitting my pitching wedge fat?

The first people to really get on top of the god dilemma were the Egyptians. The Egyptians invented gods for every conceivable situation in life - gods of love, war, hate, constipation, and on and on. All in all it worked well. It gave many men jobs as priests, who without all the gods would have had to get normal jobs like everyone else, either fighting wars or building pyramids. The rich in their idle time were sitting around thinking about ways to keep the poor down and trying to decide if there needed to be a god for money. But, how smart could they have really been? The Egyptians weren't intelligent enough to invent golf.

The Greeks carried on the Egyptian tradition and invented more gods. Life was becoming extremely complicated and more gods seemed to be

THE GOLF GOD

the answer. The Roman's carried on all the Greek gods and added a few of their own, they needed gods for incest and murder and political corruption. But, the Romans were the first truly intelligent race of people - they invented Paganica, a game that developed into modern golf.

During the Roman time there was a prophet living in the desert. He was starved, thirsty all the time, and dirty. One hot day he had a vision there was only one god. Now at least poor people were able to stop giving offerings to hundreds of gods that hadn't been doing them much good anyway - it did bum out a lot of priests who had to go out and finally get a real job. In later years it also made playing golf on Sunday a difficult task.

Life muddled along well enough until man began playing golf earnestly - religion had solved most of its problems, man had invented Catholics and was working on inventing Mormons and Protestants - but with the development of modern golf man's mind was once again thrown into the dark swirling void of unanswerable questions. How did that lucky so and so hit the ball into the trees and still have a shot at the green? How did my ball land in the middle of the fairway and hit a rock no bigger than a dime and bounce out of bounds? The questions went on and on into infinity, all without answers.

Then, miraculously, a man, his name now lost to the world, but a very wise man, was accidentally hit in the head with a golf club one of his opponents had tossed in anger. Lying on the ground he had a vision. The vision hit him harder than the golf club had and from then on he was a drunken slob who never had a job, a wife, kids, a house, and of course no mortgage payment, and spent his days playing golf. All in all he was a very happy man and envied by every golfer in the area. The truth that hit him in the head was, of course, there is another god. There is a Golf God. But, unlike the God of life, the Golf God enjoys screwing around with you, finds great satisfaction in seeing you grieve, doesn't really care if you pray or not, and loves it when you play golf on Sunday.

Until this book golfers did not know if there was truly a Golf God. Most golfers felt there was a being higher than they were but there was no proof until the Golf God appeared to me.

After reading this book you will know the reasons for all the misfortune that happens to one on a golf course: bad lies in the fairway (for real golfers only), lost balls, errant tee shots on the last hole when you have played 17 holes of the best golf of your life, plugged sand trap lies, putts that break up hill, and on and on. And please, don't despair, this book is a lot easier to read than the Bible and

THE GOLF GOD

you don't have to memorize anything.

"How did you become our God?" I asked the Golf God when he appeared to me.

He looked at me with a twinkle in his eyes. "I challenged the devil to 18 holes of match play for the souls of all golfers. After 12 holes the devil knew he had been tricked. At the time I was a solid 7 handicap and the devil was an 18. I'm no idiot. I lied about my handicap. In disgust the devil quit the match saying, "You can have all the golfers, they don't have souls anyway."

"I'll be," I said.

"The devil and I have been on speaking terms ever since," the Golf God chuckled. "He likes me, I cheat."

Before I was chosen to be the Golf God's messenger, I had in my mind the Golf God was a pious old man with long flowing sideburns who wore a kilt and enjoyed killing Englishmen while swilling scotch. But as you shall see I was wrong - extremely wrong.

I was sitting at the bar at the Fleece Muni gulping a beer and wondering who I could borrow a hundred bucks from to pay off the bet I had just lost because I had choked an 18 inch putt - being in debt to everyone on the course I couldn't figure an easy way out. A lady was sitting at the end of the bar and a strange looking man started dancing a jig on top of the bar in front of her. "You see that guy dancing on the bar," I said to Sand Trap, the bartender.

Sand Trap looked down the bar, of course saw nothing, and then leaned over and whispered in a fatherly fashion, "Shanks, you had better go home and practice your putting. When the guys come in you owe I'll tell them you went to the bathroom and will be right back."

I looked down the bar and could still see the funny looking guy dancing, but I see break in 18-inch putts so I got up and headed quickly for my car. As I approached my car I saw the dancing man sitting on the passenger side in the front seat, which is a feat in itself, because if you don't lock your car at the Fleece Muni, people you owe money to have been known to put a chain around your steering wheel. I knew I had locked my car. I am not one who is known for winning golf bets. I tried to ignore the man in my car as I put my clubs in the trunk. When I slid in behind the steering wheel the man smiled, held out his hand to shake and said, "Shanks, I have chosen you to write a book about golf that will benefit all golfers and until you make me angry you will be my only disciple."

"You really exist," I stammered. "The Golf God really exists."

Don't ask me how I knew this being was the

THE GOLF GOD

Golf God, looking back I think it was a severe case of anxiety and depression.

I saw the guys who I had lost the hundred bucks to coming out of the clubhouse with menacing looks on their faces. Sand Trap must have snitched me.

As I drove quickly through the gates of the Fleece Muni the Golf God gave me a concerned look. "You do have some beer at your house?" he asked.

I was somewhat offended but tried to keep the hurt out of my voice. "Of course I do," I replied.

"You sure choked that 18-inch putt," he said and looked worriedly out the back window.

"The guys I owe the bet to don't know where I live," I said.

The Golf God settled comfortably into the seat and smiled. "A guy who putts as bad as you do and gambles has to be extremely smart," he said, adding, "I have chosen wisely."

CHAPTER TWO
DOUBTING THOMAS

The Golf God was sitting comfortably in my recliner sipping on a cold beer. Scrutinizing the Golf God closely I don't know if I have been truly blessed or not. Looking the way he does if he had not been a god I would kick him out of my house knowing he would only leave after eating all my food and drinking all my beer.

The Golf God is a little short guy, five feet two inches at the most. He looks to be around fifty years old and has a substantial beer belly. He weighs about 150 pounds. His face is shaped like a half-inflated basketball and his eyes are big and round, but I could never tell what color they are because they were always bloodshot. His lips are set halfway between a sneer and someone who has just put one over on you, like a poker playing Santa Clause. He has a compulsion for ugly short pants in gaudy colors, white socks that do not stay up, and

THE GOLF GOD

floppy hats he can wipe the sweat off his face with. He wears old tennis shoes - he says if a golfer needs spikes he swings too hard. He has trouble shaving, having a tendency to nick himself and bleed for hours. He loves junk food, especially the hot dogs, chilidogs, and greasy hamburgers golfers gobble down between nines. He likes beer, whichever is cheapest. He likes football. He can tolerate basketball. But he can't stand bowling. There is something that sticks in his craw about a game that has no obstacles and the fact the ball comes back to you without being chased. He lives in a tiny cramped room filled with beer cans, broken golf clubs, golf books, balls fished out of water hazards and ashtrays overflowing with the unfiltered cigarettes he smokes. He has flunkies, all one-time bookies, that got a reprieve from hell to work for him - I told you he and the devil are on speaking terms. The bookies are on golf courses all over the world and with mental telepathy report to the Golf God. The Golf God sits in his kingdom and renders his judgments quickly and efficiently. Nothing escapes his flunky's vision. The Golf God does not sleep and he even has people working at all night driving ranges.

Don't ever think you can slip one by on him and never forget the Golf God loves the pained expression on your face when you are being chastised for breaking one of his rules.

"I didn't think the Golf God would look like you do," I said. "I thought the Golf God would be so proud he is almost arrogant, very handsome, and wear a kilt."

"Shanks, if a man wearing a kilt walked into the Fleece Muni and said he was the Golf God, what would you think?"

"That boy is a crazy idiot and might be dangerous," I said.

"Exactly, but for your information, I can appear to people in any form I want. I think the way I look to you fits the times, most of you golfers anymore are a bunch of slobs."

"What should I call you?" I asked the Golf God as he finished his second beer, not at all offended by his remark.

"Golf God is fine," the Golf God said. "But when you talk to me I want you to drink a beer. I do not like to drink alone."

I immediately went to the kitchen and opened a beer. "While you're in there you'd better bring me two more," the Golf God called.

I knew my twelve pack would not be enough.

Sitting down on the sofa I asked. "Just why, Golf God, did you choose me to write a book besides the fact I can't putt?"

The Golf God lit a smoke and seemed to go

THE GOLF GOD

into deep thought and after a while said. "I don't have the faintest idea."

I was shocked, mortified, deflated.

"I thought of a reason," the Golf God said seeing my despair. "I know you have one wood in your bag that is real wood and not one of those metal things even my grandmother can hit 285 yards."

"How can you call something that is metal, a wood?" I asked.

"How can you call yourselves golfers when most of you move the ball in the fairway and bitch when everything isn't perfect?" he asked, not answering my question.

I didn't have an answer and for the next few minutes we did not talk. He finished his two beers and I went to the kitchen and brought back four more. "It is not as easy being a God as you might think it is," he said between gulps of beer.

I wanted to tell him I'd change places with him but I wasn't brave enough.

"Shanks, I am going to fill you with bits of wisdom about golf that I want you to put in a book. And for doing this you can ask me a few questions about golf that will help my followers become better golfers.

I have always dreamed about writing a book, but not being able to spell or know the difference between a verb and an adjective can get in the way.

"What will I need to write your book?" I asked excitedly.

"Unless you have a photographic memory, you will need a pen and paper or a tape recorder," he said, eyeing me like I was dumber than a four putt.

I felt in awe and slightly drunk as I went to my room to get paper and pen.

Sitting back down I was almost giddy. I would be the first person in the history of golf to have his mind cleared of all obstacles, and from this day forward, I would walk down the fairway of a golf course with my head held high and a bounce to my step. In other words I was about to be blessed.

I sat, pen poised, in a rhapsody of anticipation, my every nerve on edge.

"Where is the bathroom?" The Golf God asked.

"You don't start a book that way," I said.

Twenty minutes later he returned.

I did not feel as blessed and wondered if he had a prostrate problem.

"Shanks," the Golf God said.

I poised my pen over the paper.

"Go and get us a pizza and some more beer."

"I don't have any money," I whined.

"Who cares, your luck will change, write them

THE GOLF GOD

a bad check."

As I trudged to the door to do my Lord's bidding he called to me. "Buy the cheap beer and get extra cheese on the pizza. When you get back we will start the book with the real history of golf."

Driving I tried not to be a Doubting Thomas, but I wondered if being the Golf God's disciple was such a good thing, and if his wisdom would help me win enough money to put in the bank before my check bounced? I would rather play terrible golf than be in jail.

CHAPTER THREE
THE TRUE HISTORY OF THE GAME OF GOLF

Author's note: The dictated version of the Golf God's True History of Golf was 250 pages. Due to his jerky prose and the fact he is overly verbose I took the liberty to do a major edit and paraphrased many pages of his into my own words. Please do not worry, no important information was lost.

******

The Golf God rested the pizza box on his knees and did not offer me a slice. He ate like a pig, spilling pizza sauce all down the front of his shirt and chewing with his mouth open. He is not somebody you want to take home for dinner. When he was done he opened another beer. "Now I'll tell you the real history of golf," he said like the pizza was the best meal he had eaten in years.

There was one piece of pizza left and I took a bite, wondering if he could turn the rest into thousands of pizzas to feed the world's golfers, or, at least me.

"When do I get to ask you some questions about golf that will help all golfers?" I asked in a humble voice.

"When I am good and ready to let you ask," he said gruffly, "and I don't want any interruptions while I'm telling you the real history of golf."

I took it the Golf God does not like to be messed with after he has eaten.

The Golf God began: About sixty years before the Roman's off't Jesus a group of wealthy Roman merchants and landowners were sitting around chewing the fat. They were all bored with orgies, and wine, and watching criminals and poor people being eaten by wild animals. They decided they needed a place to open up new markets so they could make more money. By making more money they figured they would not be bored - this was the beginning of multi-national corporations and capitalism. Knowing they had all the politicians in their back pockets they talked the Emperor into sending an army north. Why north? They didn't really know, but it sounded like a good idea, and being so rich and full of themselves any idea they

THE GOLF GOD

had was a good idea.

The Emperor, being wise, knew who buttered his bread. He formed an army of soldiers and approached a second rate Colonel to lead them. The Colonel had been illegally selling bows to the Huns, which the Emperor was getting a kick back on, and word was the Colonel was about to get caught. The Emperor thought it best to get the Colonel as far north as possible. The Colonel did not want to go north, but he knew his time was running out and he did not want to take a fall for the Emperor- this was before snitches were given immunity.

The Emperor sent the army and the Colonel off to conquer England, which at the time was called, The Cold Rainy Place Where The Elephants Go To Die. The Emperor told the Colonel, "don't come back any day soon and you can keep all the gold and silver you find."

He told him this to get back at the merchants and landowners that pulled his strings. When the merchants and landowners found out they had the Emperor killed. Their reasoning being, what good was a politician if you couldn't buy him. This solved the Colonel's problem and the merchants figured if they ever wanted to do an illegal arms deal the Colonel was their man.

After several years of battles not worth

remembering the army found themselves in England and Scotland. England and Scotland were not countries at the time, but it did not matter, the two peoples were so busy killing each other they didn't really bother the Roman's and the Roman army started getting bored.

To make matters worse, the merchants back in Rome forgot about the army stationed, Where The Elephants Go To Die. They were now busy jacking up the prices to get into the Coliseum and trying to stop the gladiators from free agency. And, since the dead Emperor had promised the army all the gold and silver, there was no top end to the deal.

The bored army in England and Scotland started playing a game called Paganica. Using a straight stick about three feet long with a knob on the hitting end, they beat a leather ball that was about the size of a chicken egg and stuffed with wool around the countryside. The game had originated in Rome, but instead of wool stuffed balls, the players used real pagan heads - the Colonel had banned real heads for wool stuffed balls hoping to influence the natives into telling him where all the gold and silver was. He was wise in his decision but stupid in having not figured out by looking at the local people dressed in their leather clothes, and living in cold windowless homes made of rocks and logs, that if they had any gold and

THE GOLF GOD

silver they would have figured out a way to spend it and live better lives. The only gold and silver in England and Scotland at the time was what the soldiers were wearing around their necks - gold chains being in the vogue at the time.

At this time Paganica had no rules. People just went out and happily beat the ball wherever they wanted to. It did not matter if it sliced, hooked, or if you topped it. The object was just to whack the living begedies out of the little wool ball. There was nothing to aim at, nothing to avoid, it was not a penalty to pick up the ball and place it on top of a pile of grass to hit it better. The only bad part to the game was when a player lost his ball he had to make his own ball. A private, seeing a good way to enhance his wages, started making balls for people, but after making a small fortune he got into a patent infringement case and what money he had left after paying off the lawsuit, he had to give to his lawyer.

When the Romans had finally overextended their national borders and the big corporations and landowners had run the country into the ground. Does this sound familiar? The barbarians swept in and the army had to be recalled from, Where The Elephants Go To Die. The army, overjoyed at getting to go back home, left in such haste the soldiers forgot to take all their Paganica sticks and wool stuffed leather balls. The natives, finding all the sticks and wool stuffed leather balls started playing the Roman game, Paganica, for no other reason they were too stupid to invent baseball. But, they loved the game, it was something to do with beating things with a stick.

After about 1,000 years, the English and Scots had formed into two nations, and were doing a much better job of killing each other - organization in all things helps. Although they hated each other they both enjoyed Paganica - about the only thing that had changed was the leather ball was now stuffed with feathers. The nobles on both sides frowned on the game, thinking it only a game of the rabble - this was before green fees were so high only the rich could play - and also the nobles were too busy sleeping with their own sisters to play the game. They did decide it at least kept the poor busy so they would not revolt. Let it be noted Robin Hood did not play Paganica.

Time passed, and as in most good things poor people do, one day a King stormed out of the castle after fighting with his wife and grabbed a stick from a peasant who was playing Paganica. He was about to beat the poor peasant with the stick but seeing the ball he decided to take a warm up swing. The feather filled leather ball took off like a rocket and even hooked. The peasant said, "Great shot," mainly in hopes of not getting beaten about the

THE GOLF GOD

head and shoulders.

The King was so overjoyed at his ability he made the peasant his caddie, but instead of one stick he used over fifty and he paid his caddie lousy wages.

Of course, now that the King liked the game all the other royalty liked the game - this was to become known as the King's syndrome. Rich people began beating little round leather balls filled with feathers all over the countryside. This left the poor peasants scurrying into all kinds of briar bushes, lakes, and rivers to retrieve the balls because the royalty couldn't hit the bugger straight, including the King who could no longer hit a hook because he was swinging too hard and pushing it. And, right you are, everybody played by the King's rules, which changed whenever the King wanted them to.

This system went along fine for many years until good old King James II of Scotland "banned golfe" - power trips have a way of making people idiots. King James did not like the game, he had a tremendous slice, and all his soldiers were playing too much golf and not practicing shooting their bows so they could kill Englishmen. As with all things that are banned, there were still a few brave souls who would sneak out into secluded parts of the country and hit a few, especially if the kids were fighting and the spouse was mad. Knowing if they got caught they would be killed, these brave few dug holes in the ground to hide the ball if the King's men suddenly rode up. The reasoning being, they could hide the evidence. Everybody had a stick in those days and this was before the conspiracy laws. Little did these few brave souls know the grief future generations would put upon themselves trying to get those little balls into holes.

In 1502, "the banne on golfe" was lifted with the signing of perpetual peace between England and Scotland. England could now spend its time messing with Ireland and trying to make every race in the world drink tea. There was much rejoicing and people got their illegal sticks and balls out of the closet and began madly swatting them everywhere.

The first known golf club was established in Edinburgh, Scotland in 1744. It was becoming dangerous to walk anywhere and not get hit by a flying ball, or an angrily tossed golf stick. They now had fairways, and rough, and greens - which were all sand - people not wanting grass greens until it was decided they should invent green keepers so they could have somebody to bitch at and blame their putting troubles on. With the invention of greens they also invented putters, as people needed a club to break on a regular bases.

THE GOLF GOD

Golf still had no rules, or if there were rules they were called the King's Rules, which changed as often as kings were being poisoned or beheaded.

In 1754, the grandfather of all golf clubs, THE ROYAL AND ANCIENT CLUB OF SAINT ANDREWS, was founded by a group of wealthy Scots who had to find something to fill their time with now that there were no wars, and, of course, with a name like ROYAL AND ANCIENT, they had to make rules to play the game by. They didn't like the King's Rules, because he was the only one who could cheat. There was only one main rule at the time, the ball had to be played down everywhere unless it landed in a pile of bones - there were still a few dead Englishmen laying around mixed in with the sheep that were used to cut the fairways - the founders were too cheap to higher people to mow.

As more rules were added this gave man a reason to conjure up the Golf God, who at the time, out of work, was thinking about being the God of Cricket, something he knew would bore him for eternity. It also gave a few old drunks a job of wondering around the golf course finding and selling lost golf balls.

During this time there were many changes in the stick that had been originally used to swat the feathery, all clubs had hickory shafts and there were now woods and irons, with weird names like mashie and spoon. But the first really major change in golf was not until 1848, when the old feathery ball was replaced by the "Gutty", a ball made from a glob of solid tree gum. The purists said it would ruin the game but they quickly changed their minds after they discovered how far they could smack the rubber ball.

An American, Coburn Haskell, invented the liquid center ball in 1899. Leave it to an American to try and get a little more out of a good thing. Of course, now, a smart man invented the golf bag. Until the invention of the golf bag people just carried their clubs under their arm. The modern golf bag is large enough a person can pack three days worth of clothes and enough food for a week - the 14 clubs are inconsequential - most people carry twenty clubs anyway - who cares about the rules.

Because mankind is never satisfied, clubs have gone from hickory shafts to metal shafts to graphite shafts. One day they will invent a club with no shaft that hits the ball for you. There are ten thousand different club styles, four thousand different grips, and twenty five thousand different golf balls. All of which say they are the best.

A game as easy to bet on as golf spread quickly from where The Elephants Go To Die. First to Ireland, it is also a game well suited to the abuse of

THE GOLF GOD

alcohol. It spread entirely through Europe before traveling to Canada and then the United States. It took the United States so long to catch onto the game, because they were busy killing Indians, stealing land, and developing organized crime.

In 1873, The Royal Montreal Golf Club was formed. It is the oldest club in North America. In 1888 the Saint Andrews Golf Club was formed in Yonkers, NY. In 1894, the Amateur Golf Association was formed as the governing body of golf in North America.

They were tired of the English still thinking they had won the war. It is now known as the P.G.A.

For all of these years golf was a rich man's sport. They had made so much money paying lousy wages nobody else could afford the green fees. In 1916, the pro tour was formed. The purses were not good, but since only the rich played, it did not really matter.

It was not until after WW II that the rich could no longer hold back the masses from taking up the game of golf. This was not out of the kindness of their heart, mind you They were forced by the unions to pay a wage a man could live on, something that appalled them even to this day, but it was hard to control a bunch of ex-soldiers who had been out killing, while the rich sat back in the real world making things the armies needed and got richer.

Groups of fat cats all over the country, faced with this dilemma, got together with various city fathers and said, "We get the concession and beer stand action and we'll sell you the land. You build some municipal courses for the average people to play on and you can have the green fees and pro shop money - of course the pro shops had to buy their merchandise from you know who?

All the city fathers agreed - don't forget the King's Men syndrome. Municipal courses sprang up all over the country. This helped the rich and the middle class. The poor were still stuck with being caddies.

From its humble beginnings, golf has become one of the most popular outdoor sports in the world. There are golf courses in every country. Golf courses are the melting pots, they give places for bookies, drug dealers, and other undesirables to hang out with lawyers, bankers, doctors and politicians - the legal undesirables. Nobody on a golf course cares what you do, how old you are, where you are from, if you just lived down ten for murder. All they want to know is what your handicap is and how long they can string you out before they pay if they lose a bet.

With the popularity of golf and the zillions of

THE GOLF GOD

golf courses there is now the modern P.G.A. tour. There are pros on tour from every walk of life - an accomplishment that is reached by only a fortunate few. The only way a golfer can make the tour is if on the day he was born the Golf God was feeling mellow, maybe he had had his first beer of the day, or maybe he felt guilty about making some poor 19 handicapper miss a four inch putt to break ninety. Who knows why? But, none the less, the Golf God says to the newborn: "Thou shalt be blessed by me. Thy putts will roll straight and true. Thy woods high and long. Thy chips will seek pins. Thou shall hit 2 irons out of nine-inch rough to within six feet of the pin. Thy ball will hit the rocks on the 18th hole at Pebble Beach and bounce back in bounds. Thou shall be a pro and I will give thee few problems."

But, the Golf God reneges every so often. You have seen the pro on Sunday marching down the fairway with his poor caddie half running behind him carrying a 2,000 pound golf bag that the pro has forgotten which pocket he put his Mercedes in. The pro is stalking his shot with all the calm and grace of a conquering hero. He is wearing $1,000 golf shoes, $200 dollar slacks, and a $150 dollar shirt. For the logo on his cap he is getting paid sixty big ones. For playing the clubs he is hitting he is getting another hundred grand. His golf glove is a measly fifteen thousand. The announcer is telling the world the poor guy has only made $1,400,000 on tour this year. Every so often the Golf God will say, "Na, not today."

Everybody watching sees the pro line up his shot and snap hooks the ball into the lake. Outwardly they sigh, while inwardly they rejoice knowing the pro is still human.

Don't all of us suffering golfers dream about being a pro? I can see myself in the morning kissing the little lady good-bye as I head off to practice and saying, "Hon, I'm off to the golf course, don't wait up for me, there might be a poker game tonight after work."

And, the little lady would say, gushing with love as I walk out the door with my golf clubs, "I love you dear, you are one great putter. Don't forget the mink coat or the private jet you promised me."

When the Golf God was done, he looked at me with a shine on his face as if I should prostrate myself before him.

"Are you telling me the truth?" I asked.

"Is your handicap an 8?" he asked, more piously than the Pope.

"Of course," I replied in my best golf lying face.

"Well then?" he said.

I headed for the bathroom.

CHAPTER FOUR
FREDDY AND THE BIG MATCH

"Now may I please ask you some questions that will help golfers?" I asked the Golf God trying not to sound like I was begging.

The Golf God was popping the top on another can of beer. He had consumed at least two six packs by now, but for all I could tell it had not phased him. He took two loud gulps of beer, sighed in a way so that I knew it was very hard for him to be bothered by a mere mortal, even if I was his disciple, and said, "Not yet, I am not in the mood. I want you to entertain me like a good host should and tell me the story about Freddy and the big match."

"But Golf God," I tried to protest. "You have complete knowledge of what goes on, on every golf course in the world and you had to see the drama as it happened."

"I don't care," he said. "I want you to tell me the story in your own words."

THE GOLF GOD

"Then will you let me ask you some questions about golf?" I asked.

"Maybe," he said, knowing he had all the power.

"Ok, I'll tell you the story," I said, hoping when I was finished he would at least answer one of my questions.

It is hard to deal with a God, especially one who drinks all day long. The Golf God smiled and scratched his belly in contentment.

He reminded me of a mischievous Buda.

I fondly remembered Freddy as I started the story.

******

There is a great little municipal course in the United States, to protect the guilty I will not divulge either the state or the city, but the locals call the course, The Fleece Muni. If you ever need a place to hide from the law most of the people who play there have fake I.D.'s and could care less what your real name is. If you ever want to play for money all you have to do is stand on any corner in town with your golf clubs and a hundred dollar bill stuck to your forehead. The vultures will smell you out so quickly you will have to decide which one you want to ride to the golf course with. Let me warn you though, don't get in between two of the vultures when they start fighting over new meat. It can get dangerous when pieces of cheap golf shirts start flying in different directions.

A match was set up one day between two local sticks and two old boys out of Texas. Both teams were good players, had deep pockets, and were big betters. It was rumored the Texas boys had more money than Tiger Woods. The two local sticks were so confident they were already counting their winnings, wondering if they wanted to squander it on women or flying to Vegas.

As with all the matches set up at the Fleece Muni, there had to be referees. Freddy and I were asked if we would take on the dubious honor. Freddy was a well-respected bookie - respected because it usually only took him three weeks to pay off. And, I, at the time, was a good golfer. This was before the Golf God made me suffer to see if I would be a good disciple.

Freddy was Hawaiian, with long black hair, and was extremely proud of the eight hairs he had growing on his lip he called a mustache. Most of the time he was smiling, since bookies, if they ply their trade right don't lose. Freddy dressed like he still lived in Hawaii and played golf bare-footed whenever he could. He played the ukulele and sang and dreamed about going back to Hawaii and

THE GOLF GOD

having a lounge act. But, he could never leave all the easy money behind, and he had heard the Japanese had all the action covered on The Islands. The fact his voice sounded like an old crow might also have had something to do with it. Freddy's claim to fame, though, was the fact he was one of the best cheats born to the sordid life of golf. So good, in fact, he was often asked to be a referee because it was almost impossible to put one over on him. Freddy, like a good politician, was such a likable guy that when you caught him cheating, he would stand there with a jack-o-lantern grin on his face as if he was trying to sell you a string of seashells, and you would start feeling guilty for catching him. Freddy was one talented guy.

To be a referee for a major golf bet at the Fleece Muni one had to do more than ride around in a cart and guzzle beer. Besides watching for cheating, you have to carry a ball bat, either to enforce your decisions, break up a fight, or for your own protection. You also have to be trustworthy enough not to take a bribe. Freddy and I could not figure out a way to take a bribe from both teams, believe me, we tried.

We were standing on the first tee and the two local sticks and the Texas boys were going through the normal golf talk while they tried to size each other up. I checked to make sure no one had more than the 20-club limit that had been agreed upon, there was no Vaseline on the towels, and no one had a ball bat except me. (If you did not know a thin layer of Vaseline on the face of a club will make the ball go farther)

Freddy checked the golf balls to make sure they were legal sized and not one of those illegal balls that goes about 600 yards. I looked at the individual marks on each ball. Satisfied everything was honest up to this point, although it's hard to cheat on the tee box, I flipped a coin and the Texas boys won the toss.

The match was set up as team low ball, $5,000 on each nine per player, with a chance to press to get even on holes 9 and 18.

If a team was down after eight holes they would play the last hole for double or nothing.

If the team that was down won, they were even, if they lost, they lost $10,000 a man on the front nine. Starting on the 10th hole they would be playing the back nine for $5,000. If the team that had lost the front also was down going into the last hole, they could double the front nine bet and double the last nine bet - which means if they won the last hole they were even for the day. If they pushed they lost $15,000, and if they lost, they lost $30,000. You might see more of our pro's choking if they played for their own money.

THE GOLF GOD

Freddy was nervous as the match began because he had side bets with a lot of the local vultures that thought the Texas boys would kick some tail. I didn't have any side bets because I was coming off a sound stomping the Sunday before and hadn't been able to find anybody I could borrow any money from. I had even tried my mother.

There is no need to get into the majority of the match which, like the majority of golf on TV it was boring. The two local sticks were $10,000 down after nine holes. The scotch they guzzled after nine holes did not help a bit as they were four down on the back nine with three holes to play. Since the local boys were four down with three holes to play we skipped holes 16 and 17 and drove over to the 18th tee box, cutting in front of a foursome, who didn't care a bit as they had heard about the match and enjoyed the pained faces of the two local sticks - the local sticks had cleaned their plow earlier in the week for fifty bucks each.

On the 18th tee one of the local sticks said in a shaking voice, "We double the amount." Which meant the last hole was worth $30,000.

I watched the Texas boys smile at each other. I also noticed a guy, the local sticks must have hired, walk to their car in the parking lot and start it. They had a signal I did not catch. A sad part of being a referee is you have to make sure the winners get paid and I could see myself chasing the local sticks through the parking lot with the ball bat. I knew Freddy wouldn't help, he would be high tailing to get away from all the guys he was going to owe. He wasn't stupid. Freddy had parked his car at a grocery store several blocks away. It goes without saying Freddy was not a happy camper. He knew he couldn't hide forever and there is nothing a bookie hates more than having to pay. You can't lay off golf bets.

The 18th hole is a rather short par four, 400 yards long, with a slight dog leg right. The fairway slopes to the right and is only about 30 yards wide. There is a large trap on the right side that eats golf balls. The locals call the trap, The Turkey, because it is good at gobbling up balls. A good drive will end up even with the trap. But, a cut or pushed drive, the ball ends up in the bunker or worse yet, in ankle deep grass that grows to the right of the bunker.

There is a driving range that runs along the left side of the fairway that is O.B. There is an old man who rents a cart and has a football helmet, and if he is around he will put the helmet on, and for a dollar, ride out and get your golf ball. When he does go in for a ball everyone on the range aims for him. It's like watching a rabbit trying to dodge hailstones.

THE GOLF GOD

The green is small, kidney shaped, and has two bunkers in front of it. It is slightly elevated. The parking lot is ten yards behind the green and is O.B. The green is always hard, the green keeper's wife ran away with a golfer and he has never gotten over it, so it takes an extremely high shot to hold the green and not bounce over. Because of this, a wood has to be hit off the tee - a long iron shot will not hold the green.

The first Texan got up and snap hooked his ball O.B. into the driving range. The guy with the football helmet drove out onto the range, dodged about fifty golf balls, found the ball and put it in his pocket. I've heard the old man is an ex-marine and still needs action to feel alive.

The second Texas boy pushed his drive but the ball cleared the bunker and landed in the tall grass. Freddy muttered, "I wish he had hit it in the driving range."

The two local sticks felt better. The Texas boy, even if he found the ball, had a tough shot. Both of the local sticks got off good drives, one left center and one right down the middle. Freddy was feeling much better after the drives but not good enough to give me more than a forced grin as we headed down the fairway.

After looking for several minutes we could not find the Texas boy's ball in the tall grass by the bunker. Both Texas boys were looking frantically. Freddy was also looking, but not very hard. The two local sticks were standing in the fairway looking at their watches, five minutes was going to be it, but they sure as hell weren't going to help look for the ball.

Like I said, the grass behind the bunker is ankle deep, and balls do get lost there, but I had not lost sight of the ball all the way from the tee. I was looking back at the tee, double checking the ball flight when the Texas boy called out happily, "Here it is I found it."

I checked the ball, and sure enough it was his ball, markers and all. To top it off the ball had one of the best lies I had ever seen in the tall grass. Of course I checked to see that there was no tee under the ball.

As Freddy and I headed for our cart Freddy looked like he had lost his best friend, which was impossible, as Freddy had no true friends. As we sat in the cart Freddy said to me in a voice that sounded like a frog that had just been run over by a Mac truck, "That cheatin' dog, that no good lyin' pig."

"Who?" I asked.

"That boy from Texas," Freddy croaked.

"What do you mean?" I asked seriously, reaching for the ball bat.

THE GOLF GOD

"That can't be his ball," he half cried, holding his head in his hands as though it weighed a ton.

"Why not?" I demanded.

"I got his ball in my pocket," he whimpered as the boy from Texas stuck his iron shot not more than six inches from the hole.

I looked toward the parking lot and the two local sticks man was still sitting in the car. Two men, who looked like professional wrestlers, walked up to the car, and one with a large smile on his face reached into the car and turned off the ignition. The other waved at the two Texas boys who happily waved back.

When I turned to look at Freddy he was already hotfooting toward the grocery store.

The Golf God laughed so hard he spurted a swallow of beer all over the living room. "Freddy, Freddy," he said when he could finally talk. "When he dies he will be a good worker for me."

CHAPTER FIVE
WHAT IS THE SECRET TO PUTTING?

"Ok, ok, I have told you the story about Freddy, now would you answer a question for me?" I asked in a tone letting the Golf God know it was his turn to live up to his promise.

"Is there any more beer?" The Golf God asked me with a tad bit of worry in his voice. "And potato chips if you have any."

I brought him back a beer and a bag of stale potato chips. "These are great," he grinned, after stuffing his mouth with a fist full of chips and letting the crumbs fall all over his shirt. "Now what is your question?"

"You mean you will really answer a question?" I sputtered in surprise.

"Shanks, do you think I would lie to you?" The Golf God asked looking like an altar boy that had drank the priest's hidden stash of real wine.

THE GOLF GOD

"No, no, never," I replied doing my best to sound like I was telling a white lie.

The Golf God smiled.

I leaned forward on the sofa and looked at the Golf God with my most reverent eyes, cleared my throat, and could feel his warm glow of enlightenment about to enter my soul. "What is the secret to putting?" I asked, visualizing the shocked look of my next opponent as I sank every treacherous three footer.

The Golf God's eyes bulged out, his cheeks swelled up to double their normal pudgy size, and he blew a cloud of half chewed and beer soaked potato chips halfway across the room. "What, what," he stammered. "You dare ask me about putting?"

"But you are the Golf God," I almost sobbed.

The Golf God leaned back in the chair and placed his hand over his heart, like he has one, and took several deep breaths.

"You don't know everything," I said, letting the full force of my disappointment hang in the air like the pleas from a man with a 20 handicap with a buried lie in the road hole bunker at Saint Andrews.

"Listen Shanks," the Golf God said in a low and far away voice. "Back in the days of Paganica there was no such things as putters. A man merely hit the ball and chased it. It was a fun game then, an outlet for stress. Modern man, overloaded with the need to succeed, needs tortuous levels of stress to feel worthy so some idiot invented the putter.

I felt like the Golf God was evading my question but I did not butt in. It is not the place for a disciple to butt in on his God, no matter if he cannot answer a simple question, and I still clung to a feeble amount of hope he could tell me the secret to putting.

"I know a guy who has made a good living fixing broken putters he finds," the Golf God continued. "He has found putters in the urinals of locker rooms, wrapped around ball washers, and he has found six putters in one tree by a particularly tough green. He has found putters in parking lots, garbage cans, and on the roofs of clubhouses. From one water hazard in front of a very difficult 18th hole he has fished out 17 putters. To date he has found over 2,500 putters. Figure it out, 2,500 times the fifty bucks he sells them for is my idea of a good job."

The Golf God took swig of beer, lit a smoke, and seemed to settle into a mood of deep thought before saying. "Shanks, the golfer has a love/hate relationship with his putter. When a person is putting well they are a happy camper. The putter is better than a honeymoon, better than a steak dinner,

THE GOLF GOD

better than a month long vacation. But when the putter goes bad, watch out. Golfers will beat the dog, yell at the spouse, and sooner or later the putter is going to get some airtime. But through it all it will never be the golfer's fault - it will always be the putter's fault. Golfers are extremely good at denial and making up lame excuses as to why they can't putt."

My enlightenment was fading quickly as the Golf God lit another smoke from the still burning butt of the one he had.

"Most golfers own one or two putters," the Golf God said. "And as you know they come in every shape and size imaginable, from the traditional blade putter to putters that look like they belong on the nose cone of a missile. Putters also have more names than there are broken tees on a nine-hole course in Iowa."

"I know, I know," I beseeched the Golf God. "Just tell me the secret." Even a disciple can run out of patience when it comes to matters as important as putting.

The Golf God ran his tongue over his lips nervously, looked at the ceiling, finally shook his head from side to side, and mumbled, "I can't tell you."

My faith started to run out the door like a thief making off with your TV set. "You can't tell me,"

I croaked. "I am your chosen one, and you can't tell me?"

The Golf God shook his head sadly and blurted out, "part of my divorce settlement was I had to promise I would never, never, help anyone putt. I can only help people three putt."

"You mean I am lost forever," I cried in anguish.

"Knowing my ex-wife you are more than lost," the Golf God said in a tone I knew there was no hope.

"Does your ex-wife need a disciple?" I asked hopefully.

"Shanks, my ex likes expensive wine, nice clothes, the opera. You couldn't afford her. And besides, if she ever finds out you talked to me you won't ever two putt another green in your life."

"Isn't there a way to talk to the judge and change your settlement?" I beseeched.

"The judge is a bowler," the Golf God said in a tone that sounded like he was gagging.

"Oh, Golf God," I moaned.

"You learn to live with it," the Golf God said. "My ex has told me that if I would take up bowling she would let me help people putt."

"You can't do that," I said in disgust.

"I know," the Golf God said. "There are some things one cannot stoop to."

THE GOLF GOD

"Oh, Golf God," I moaned again.

"Get us another beer," the Golf God told me.

Now I understand why the Golf God drinks so much.

The Golf God drank his beer in silence. After a few minutes he looked at me with a twinkle in his eye and said, "If I could have told you the secrets to putting you wouldn't have told the world anyway."

I started to say, "of course I would have," but I can't lie that good.

"Don't worry about it Shanks," the Golf God said. "I'll tell you how to make a good bet."

"If you can't putt there is no such thing as a good bet," I replied utterly dejected.

The Golf God pondered this for a moment and then leaned toward me. "I can tell you one thing about putting," he whispered.

I still might be saved. I leaned toward him until my face was an inch from his. "Yes, tell me," I said almost in tears.

"You have to know when to lag," he said so softly I could barely hear him.

I started to speak, but he put his hand over my mouth. I could see fear in his bloodshot eyes. His ex-wife must truly be one tough lady.

CHAPTER SIX
HOW TO MAKE A GOOD BET

"Let's be honest with ourselves," the Golf God said. "For all the mystique people have showered on golf, for all the gentlemen's game rhetoric we have all been taught, and for all the love of the game we tell each other, in all truth, most golfers have more larceny in them than any other sport. The main reason most people play golf is to gamble - whether you play for ten cents a hole or $10,000. The worst thing is, to get an even bet in golf is harder to do than hit the lottery. Golf has a handicap system that makes it possible for a guy who can't hit the ball out of his shadow, never lands on the green, and hasn't made a putt in three years, to beat the pants off a good player and then brag about it. Does this make any sense to you?"

I started to answer but he raised his hand and I knew he didn't want an answer, but I had drunk enough beer I was getting brave and I said. "When

THE GOLF GOD

I started playing for money I was thrashed for a month by guys I could beat with one hand. I was utterly dismayed by the idea I was going to have to go and get a job until an old hustler saved me. Being old he was getting sentimental and figured he had better convey some of his wisdom to people who needed it before he died. Besides, he had plied his trade so well he couldn't get any bets unless he went to Pago Pago. He came up to me, put his talon for a hand on my shoulder, looked me in the eyes with his, don't give me any excuses why you can't pay me eyes, and said, "Son, if you are in this for the money don't make a bet you can't win."

"Exactly," the Golf God smiled. "That is exactly it. Now I want to give you three very important pointers about gambling before I get into the art of negotiating a bet."

First: Make sure you are like all the other lying bums who gamble and jack up your handicap. And if you are shooting a round far below your handicap you had better blow out a big hole. An honest man, with an honest handicap, will get his honest rear end beat nine out of ten times.

Second: Don't ever be fair in a game of golf. If you want to be fair in life then become a monk, and if anybody ever says to you, "well that's not a fair bet," he is the biggest thief in the crowd.

Third: Etch this in your mind - don't play if you

can't pay.

"That's good advice," I said ignoring my inadequacies at paying off golf bets.

"Ok, Shanks, now I will tell you how to negotiate a bet."

My ears perked up, my heart pounded in my chest like I was a Jamaican bongo player who had been smoking pot non-stop for three days while drinking two gallons of dark rum.

"A group of guys are all mingling around the putting green looking for a game and sizing each other up," the Golf God began. "They are waiting for someone to make the first move and start negotiating a bet. Most bets are mainly team bets, two against two, three against three, or four against four, its an ego thing, team members can always blame the other player when a team does badly. Because of this everybody is looking to see who they can get on their side to really stack the bet in their favor - remember what I said about being fair in this game. Finally one of the group will ask, "are we going to play golf or not?"

This will be met with head nods and people inching closer to the guys they want to play with. "I will take Jim, Bill and Mark," somebody will say who wants everybody to think he is not trying to stack his team.

But the first offer is always wrong. Etch this in

THE GOLF GOD

your mind. The first offer is always wrong. There are no exceptions.

After the first offer there is always the endless list of golfer's excuses why their game has in one way or another gone to hell recently.

"I haven't been putting well." This line is always said by the guy who makes the 95 footer once a round and hasn't three putted in ten years.

"My shoulder hurts, I had to mow the yard." This guy hasn't mowed a yard in over fifteen years - he hires the neighbor kid.

"My back is hurting." Like a bunch of golfers really care if your back hurts. Tell it to your doctor, which he won't do, because the doctor will tell him to stop playing golf for a month.

"I haven't played in three weeks." Two guys saw the bum playing at another course and another guy saw him practicing at an all night driving range.

"My hay fever is acting up and I am having a hard time breathing." Then go to the movies.

"You guys are too good for us." This line is always used by the best player on the course.

"The last time we played you guys you beat us." So what, the last time we played you guys shot the worst round you have ever shot, and how about the fifteen times you beat us before that. Golfers have extremely short memories when they win, extremely long memories when they lose.

"Well my handicap is 12 and yours is 2." If you base your bets on handicap you deserve to lose.

Besides all the verbal excuses you see guys limping, rubbing their shoulders, holding their heads, pretending their eyes hurt, and checking to see if they still have hands. All of these ailments seem to go away with the first swing.

When all the excuses have been used up there is always a few moments of silence before the next counter offer for teams. "Well, I'll take so and so and so and so, and you give so and so three shots."

Counter: "Do you want to get paid now and just forget golf?"

"Ok, then, I'll take so and so and so and so and you give us two shots."

Counter: "I wouldn't give my mother two shots."

"You guys don't want to play golf." This is normally said by a guy both teams want on their side with a hint he might not play. Don't worry, he will play, he wouldn't have driven all the way to the golf course just to turn around.

When the teams are finally arranged you now have to decide what you are going to play for. "We'll play you for two chickens, a duck, and your house."

Chickens and ducks are fine if you have the edge. Who cares about the house let them have the

THE GOLF GOD

mortgage.

Normally the team that has the advantage will want the bet to be higher. Be wary if you throw out a ridiculously high bet and the opposing team takes it without a gripe. This is only done when they have pulled in a ringer. The ringer being the guy who all during the excuses and team choosing did not say a word, only stood around and looked dumb, like he is out of his element and doesn't feel comfortable on a golf course. The, I don't play much guy. Yea, you bet, he is the guy that lives by a golf course, has a putting green in his back yard, and makes his own clubs.

Now that the teams have been chosen and the bet set, each team goes to a neutral corner and goes through a pep talk. "We can beat them into the ground."

"Let's do it."

"If we lose this one we are a bunch of dogs."

It doesn't matter if some of the guys on the other team are your best friends, your father, or married your sister, it's still, "Let's bury them."

After all it is a war. The only thing different is golfers don't have Geneva Convention Cards.

Another thing you should do before a match is make sure everybody has money to pay if you win and never take a check.

After the round the winning team will always

say, "Let's go again."

"What do you mean?" you should say. "You just kicked our tails from here to Guatemala and back."

"You should have won," they say.

"Ok, give us four shots."

"You have to be crazy," they will say.

Always ask the first time for more shots than you need and then settle for less. But, don't forget, maybe they missed a few shots on purpose during the first round.

"I don't think anything you have said will help me," I told the Golf God.

"I know what will," he said.

"What?" I asked.

"Just go out and play the game. Learn to enjoy it. Don't bet."

I have never been one to follow good advice.

CHAPTER SEVEN
HEART AND THE PRIEST

The Golf God had been in the bathroom for over thirty minutes. I was about to doze off when he wheezed back into the living room. "You should stop smoking," I told him.

"Disciple," he said gruffly. "You should mind your own business. Besides, I can't get cancer, I am already dead."

Good logic has no argument.

Instead of telling me to go get him a beer the Golf God went to the kitchen and got his own beer and made himself a peanut butter sandwich without asking me if I wanted one. I suppose disciples are supposed to go out onto the golf course and get their own manna.

"You have to tell me another story," the Golf God said as he took a bite of sandwich.

"Which one?" I asked. I knew there was no need to argue when he wanted to be entertained.

"The one about Heart and the Priest," he replied, having eaten the sandwich in three bites and now slurping on a beer.

I didn't bother to ask him when I would be able to ask him another question.

******

The first time I met the Priest I was eating breakfast at the Fleece Muni with a bunch of the local sharks. The sharks were up earlier than usual hoping to find some fresh meat that did not know their faces. A jovial looking man sat down with us. He had on baggy red slacks with cuffs, rubber soled golf shoes that looked like he had dug them out of a dumpster, and a wrinkled pink golf shirt with a few bleach spots on it. He was not more than 5'7" tall, half-bald, with dark smiling eyes and he had to be in his early 60's. I figured out right away he was a hustler. In truth, he was not a hustler, he was a Catholic priest who loved the game of golf and loved dearly to play for enough money to tempt himself with all kinds of sins. His favorite game was two down automatics. For the sake of the Priest and the sanctity of the Catholic Church, I will say we only played for $5.00 a bet - $5.00 is more than

THE GOLF GOD

most church people leave in the collection plate.

One of the sharks at the table was a man in his late 50's named Heart. Heart looked like a boxer who should have taken up swimming. His nose had been broken so many times from fist fights that when he talked it sounded like he had a cold. Over the past thirty years he had hustled golf all over the country. He was a scratch golfer, but he had a heart condition, thus his name. He had to carry nitro in his pocket. He was also a chronic liar, which, on a golf course never hurt anybody, but in truth he really did have a heart condition. It was not a lie to make you feel sorry for him and give him a few shots.

It was Heart's dream to die on a golf course and he was doing everything in his power to do so, which sometimes included sleeping at night on the green on the sixth hole. The greens keeper said, "If the sprinkler system coming on at night doesn't bother him I don't care."

The only water that would bother Heart was if it was in his drink.

Another shark at the table was my old friend Freddy the bookie, who by now had made enough money on basketball to regroup the whipping he had taken when the two local sticks had been thrashed by the Texas boys.

While the Priest ordered a cup of coffee I could

see Freddy and Heart snapping their jaws and trying to stop from drooling.

The other sharks at the table got up and left without even saying good bye. They had seen four men walk into the coffee shop they had never seen and they wanted to be the first to chum the water.

I will not put you through the two hours of dickering we went through to negotiate the bet, but after a debate that made the U.N. look like child's play, it was decided the Priest and I would play Freddy and Heart best ball, two down automatic presses, for $5.00, and the Priest would get three shots. If you have never played two down automatic presses you understand a seemingly small $5.00 bet can turn into a lot of money if you are playing badly.

I was flush at the time after getting a car lot owner for some major bucks. I figured it would be wise to give a few dollars back and recharge my karma. It is also smart to take on an uphill bet every so often to let the boys know you are not afraid of them. But, also in the back of my mind was the idea the Priest was in cahoots with Freddy and Heart and he was going to dump me for 1/3 of their winnings - money has a way of corrupting religion.

We decided that if the weather turned bad after the sixth hole the match would stand and the loser would have to pay. This is a good point to

THE GOLF GOD

remember. Let's say you are down going into a cut off hole and the weather looks like it will get bad, you can play slow. On the other hand, if you are up, you can play fast. I have seen golf carts doing 90 mph on a cut off hole and some mysteriously break down. Once, I had a guy down on a bet and it took him fifteen minutes to tie his shoe.

When the match started it was one of those days the Golf God was messing with me. I couldn't hit the ball straight to save the Priest's soul. If I had been putting at a manhole cover I would have missed. I couldn't even get the ball in the ball washer without it going out of bounds. The Priest, bless his no taking a dive soul, could do no wrong. He made a legitimate par on the 1st hole. He birdied the 2nd hole using one of his shots. He had another legitimate par on the 3rd hole. And he birdied the 4th hole with another one of his shots. I made par on the 5th hole with a chip in from thirty yards, which was a good thing because the Priest was laying seven when he picked up. To go along with our good luck the Priest had another shot coming on the 8th hole. We had Freddy and Heart five ways down, with a five way press going into the 6th hole, and since the weather was good there was no way we wouldn't finish if Freddy and Heart tried to stall for five or six hours.

Heart and Freddy were foaming at the mouth.

Instead of the sharks eating the tuna, the tuna had turned out to be barracuda in disguise. Heart and Freddy were telling each other, in no uncertain terms, how bad the other one was playing without putting any blame on themselves. This is a trait golfers learn early and a trait that carries over into real life. You notice when a large company goes down, it is never the fault of the big shots, the guy parking cars gets fired.

The 6th hole is a short straightaway par five that with any drive close to 250 yards there is a chance to get on the green in two. The fairway is hard and wide and the green has no bunkers in front of it. The Priest hit his drive dead center down the middle and walked off the tee looking like he had converted a Baptist. I hit my drive slightly left, but long, with at most a five wood to the green.

Freddy, grim faced, pushed his drive over into the right rough. The Priest nodded at me letting me know he would make sure Freddy did not move his ball in the rough. He knew Freddy was a sinner and could care less about any Golf God.

It was Heart's turn to hit, but he was in his cart with his head rolled back, tears were streaming down his face, and he was clutching his chest with his hand. We all ran back to him and I got the nitro bottle from his pocket and stuck one in his mouth. We knew he was truly sick as Freddy had started

THE GOLF GOD

the hole. When the nitro hit, Heart's eyes shot open and he smiled faintly. We all thought he was about to get his wish and die on the golf course. Instead, Heart, hustler that he was, and scorning our pleas to stay seated and rest, stood up and staggered to the tee and with great difficulty teed up his ball. With tears still streaming from his eyes, and a pain filled grimace on his face, Heart hit his drive about 50 feet. I thought it was a great last tribute to a golfer, one that almost made me cry. But, then I reconsidered, I've seen that bastard birdie from there.

We watched in silence as Heart staggered back towards his cart, waiting for him to fall to the ground dead. The Priest and I were sad because we knew if Heart died one of us would not get paid after all our hard work.

Heart was almost to his cart when he keeled over onto his face. It reminded me of the good bandit getting shot in the back. We all rushed over and I rolled him onto his back and held up his head. I thought there was a slim chance, that in his dying breath, he would tell me how he hit his 3 iron so good. Heart was still breathing, but his face was as pale as if he had missed a one-foot putt for all the money.

The Priest looked down at Heart and in a saintly voice asked, "Heart, are you a Catholic?"

The Priest had all the intentions of giving Heart his last rights.

Heart blinked his tearing eyes, ran his dry tongue over his lips, and said in a low raspy voice, "Hell no, Catholics never helped me putt."

The Priest held out his hand to Heart and said, "Then you pay me before you die."

Freddy started to turn all colors of blue trying to think of an excuse to stop the match, but there was none. They had both started the hole. He looked at his stricken partner and then beseechingly at the Priest and me, and said in a voice filled with doom, "you mean you guys expect me to play both of you?"

The question was so stupid we didn't even bother to answer.

"I'll play the hole by myself then," Freddy said. He knew he would have done the same if one of us was dying so there was only a slight hint of disdain in his voice.

Without another word we left Heart lying on the tee box and drove off to finish the hole. The Priest followed Freddy to make sure he did not tee up his ball in the rough, a deed Freddy would have no qualms about doing, especially since his partner might be dead.

The Priest made par. I birdied. Freddy, angry that Heart would be so stupid on his dying legs to start the hole, got a bogey.

We then drove frantically back to the tee box where another foursome was now administering to Heart. The Priest pushed his way through the men and looked down at Heart. "Heart," he said. "You owe me 50 bucks."

"I figured," Heart said weakly, handing the priest $50.00 that he already had in his hand. "That damn Freddy is never good under pressure."

The match was then cancelled, an ambulance was called, and after Heart was taken away we all went to the clubhouse to try and figure out another bet.

Three days later Heart was back from the hospital. But, never again would he give the Priest three shots. And, Freddy never forgave Heart for starting the sixth hole when he knew he didn't have a chance in hell to get home in two.

CHAPTER EIGHT
ALL THE QUESTIONS YOU WANT TO ASK

"All right, all right, I want you to answer a question that will help us suffering golfers," I told the Golf God in a firm voice, "and no excuses, you promised."

"Shanks," the Golf God said, like he didn't know or care what a promise is. "You can ask all the questions you want."

"I can?" I replied like some kid who had asked to use the car and his Dad told him yes but make sure he was back within a week.

"But when you are done I don't want to hear another question out of your mouth," the Golf God said firmly.

I started to protest but the Golf God pointed a finger at me the way my mother used to so I kept my mouth shut. He then chugged on his beer, looked at me, arched his eyebrows, and said, "Well, are you going to ask me a question or not?"

"What is the easiest way to play the ball out of a trap?" I asked quickly.

The Golf God looked at me like I was dumber than a pooper scooper, shook his head sadly, looked up at the ceiling, chewed on his lip, rubbed his head, and finally said. "Don't hit the ball in the trap is the easiest way."

"What kind of advice is that?" I cried.

"Don't mess with me Shanks," the Golf God said. "You'd better ask all the questions you can before my mood changes and you'd better phrase your questions correctly."

"How can golfers improve their chipping?" I asked quickly.

The Golf God smiled at me. I felt elated. "Most important of all, you have to accelerate through the ball on all chips, use a club that will get the ball on the green as soon as possible and run the ball to the hole."

I started to ask another question but the Golf God looked at me in a way that I knew his mood had changed. It was like he had a par round going and triple bogeyed the 18th hole or he has a terrible chemical imbalance. "I tell you what Shanks," the Golf God said. "Instead of me sitting through an endless barrage of your questions I am going to

THE GOLF GOD

give you some advice you can pass on to my followers."

I knew there was no use in protesting. "Speak on, old wise one," I said sarcastically. So far most of the information the Golf God had passed on to me would not rattle a small paper sack.

The Golf God was concentrating on opening another beer and did not catch my sarcasm.

He began in a tone of voice that reminded me of a tired college physics professor who was stuck trying to teach football players how to follow a snap count.

I have taken the liberty to put his advice into a list. I didn't think the burps and belches and the countless trips he took to the bathroom were worth mentioning.

FINALLY, TIPS FROM THE GOLF GOD

1) Take a lesson. There is a big difference in people thinking they know something and knowing.

2) Your first choice in club selection is normally your best choice. Trust your instincts - that is if you have any.

3) Aim your iron shots at the center of the green, forget where the pin is for a few rounds. After you have done this for a while, and your confidence is up, then aim at some pins.

4) When you hit in the rough your first thought should be to get the ball back into play.

5) On long putts imagine the hole is a garbage can lid and try and get your ball close to the lid. If you are a good reader of break you should remember my putting tip - know when to lag. (He said this with a whisper in case his ex-wife was listening.)

6) Get to know your golf course. Chances are you play the same course every week. Learn it. You should be able to look at any landmark and know how far it is to the green. Take the guesswork out of your shots.

7) If you are going to lay up, then lay up.

8) Don't try and hit a shot you cannot hit.

9) Play your own game. Don't think about what the other person is doing, unless you want him to hit your ball also.

10) I had to read his lips when he told me this one: When you are putting don't try and be so exact. Imagine a line running on either side of the hole and try to keep your ball inside the two lines. The hole is over four inches wide.

11) Listen to your own advice - normally a

THE GOLF GOD

person does not lie to himself or herself.

12) Play at your own pace but not a snail's pace.

14) Do not carry a cell phone on the course. If you do you might as well have stayed at the office or have a desk made you can put on the back of your cart.

15) Play the ball down. You will be surprised how well you hit it and you will learn more shots.

16) Learn where to miss. Think about this statement - this is a great tip - but one that takes a few brain cells to figure out.

17) Unless you are playing in a tornado don't aim your shot off the green.

18) Play the brand of ball you are comfortable with. They are all round and only go where you hit them.

19) Carry the legal amount of clubs. If you are a golfer then be a golfer. If you have over the legal limit then open up a shop for used golf clubs.

20) Play by the rules. (The Golf God laughed on this one)

21) Simplify...simplify....simplify...

22) Don't think, do.

23) Walk the course once in a while, a person plays better when their feet are on the ground - although it is hard to carry a six pack and a hot dog while lugging a golf bag.

24) There are no excuses unless you still suck

your thumb.
25)   Swing easy, let the club do the work.
26)   And last but not least - have fun, enjoy yourself, smile - remember golf is an individual game and nobody else cares what you do.

I was in awe. "It all seems so simple," I said with admiration smeared all over my face.

"I think I told you that," the Golf God said, "listen better."

"Thank you for all the tips," I said.

"You can thank me by getting me another beer," he replied.

I went to the kitchen a happy man, at times life is good.

"We better take the winter tires off the cart."

CHAPTER NINE
MONTANA

"Ok, tell me a story," the Golf God ordered.

"You could be more polite," I said.

"I could make you shoot 90 forever."

Gods have a way of getting their point across.

"How about the story about Montana?" I said in an appeasing tone.

"That will be fine," the Golf God said.

As I began the story I thought about Montana and felt a momentary pang of sadness.

******

It was raining and Heart the Priest and I were sitting in the coffee shop at the Fleece Muni looking out the window at the deserted putting green. Freddy, thinking we didn't know, was out on the golf course planting golf balls in the rough with his

THE GOLF GOD

mark on them. During a match if he hit in the rough, and if nobody was watching, he would play one of the planted balls. There is a large car lot that borders the Fleece Muni and a car salesman had seen Freddy crawling over the fence with bulging pockets and he called the Priest. The car salesman was a Catholic. It was not a new trick for Freddy, also one that would not work, as before the next match with Freddy, I would put my own mark on his ball - unless of course he was my partner. One thing could be said about Freddy, he tried every trick in the book more than once, his thinking being, just because I got caught last time doesn't mean they'll catch me this time - perseverance can pay off.

Heart had not had any heart attacks lately and he had been playing extremely well and was in an expansive mood - winners are always happy. The Priest was slightly bummed out. He had forgotten about a wedding he had to perform in two days and had to drop out of a match with Heart as his partner against two guys who might as well have paid before they teed up. It didn't seem fair to him, especially since the two pigeons were Lutherans. I was wishing the rain would let up as I had spent an hour wrapping my putter grip with gauze tape and wanted to try it out. "The only thing bad about that," Heart said, "is when you go to toss your putter in disgust the gauze might stick to your hand and the club will swing down and hit you in the leg."

"I didn't think of that," I said.

The pro of the course came over to the table, what with the rain he was not able to go out and make his Lincoln payment by giving lessons. The pro always reminded me of a scarecrow. For this story I will call him Snake. He was a little skinny guy about 60 years old. He smoked five packs of Pall-Malls a day and ran three miles every afternoon. His trademark was that he wore pants that were two sizes too big for him. At the Fleece Muni the wind blows most of the time and whenever one of Snake's opponents had an important putt Snake would stand close to him so all the guy could hear was Snake's pants flapping in the wind.

"I like that," the Golf God said.

Snake sat down. "Montana is coming to town," he said casually to Heart.

I had never seen Heart look so sad. His lips sagged so far they almost fell off his face.

"The poor soul," the Priest said shaking his head.

Snake smiled. He did not have to say, easy money, it was written all over his face.

Freddy came in soaking wet and sat down.

THE GOLF GOD

"My car broke down and I had to walk over," he lied.

"When is Montana getting in?" Heart asked Snake, ignoring Freddy as Freddy had lost face by getting caught.

Freddy got so excited his clothes started to dry right in front of my eyes.

"What is it with this guy Montana?" I asked, if he was really easy money I needed some, my rent was due in a week.

"Montana owns a golf course in North Dakota, when it freezes up there he always comes here for a few weeks before he heads to Vegas. He is one hell of a stick," Snake said.

I saw my rent money flying away.

"He only has one problem," Snake continued. "He has the worst case of the putting yips I have ever seen."

"The worst," the Priest said and made the sign of the cross.

"The worst," Heart said.

"The worst," Freddy said.

Nobody, even a shark who would take money from his mother, likes to see a man with the yips. In the game of golf there is nothing more excruciating than the yips. But, if you play this game long enough, in time, you will have them at least once. When you do, you will think it is the end of the world. I have seen guys with the yips line up a putt and when they finally hit the ball it goes at a right angle to the hole. With the yips a six-inch putt seems like 52 miles over the top of the Alps.

"He is bringing a guy with him I played with in Vegas several times," Snake said.

"Can we handle him?" Heart asked.

Snake nodded his head, which did not mean anything, Montana might have paid him to lie. For all we knew the guy he was bringing down could have just lost his tour card.

"Is Montana going to call again?" Heart asked.

Snake nodded his head. As you can tell Snake did not talk much. It had something to do with the five packs of Pall-Malls he smoked a day.

"Tell him Buckshot and I will play them for $1,000 a man, nassau," Heart said.

Before my name was Shanks they used to call me Buckshot for the way I sprayed the ball all over the course but seemed to manage a good score.

I started to protest. "I'll back you," Freddy said.

"What's the split?" I asked cautiously, Freddy is like a car salesman, you only think you get a good deal.

"60/40," Freddy said. "60 for me, 40 for you."

For Freddy to offer such a deal must have thought it was a no lose situation. "Fine," I said,

THE GOLF GOD

looking out the window and seeing the rain had stopped. How could I turn down a bet when I didn't have to put up the money? It made me feel like a pro. But as I left the table I saw Snake smiling.

A week later Montana was in town and the match was set. We were going to play at the country club, Montana owning a golf course could get on about any course he wanted.

The day of the match Heart picked me up at my apartment in his Cadillac. He did not want me driving my 15-year-old truck to the Country Club. Heart had a big thing about image. He even had one of those big leather bags pros have, unlike most of us who had old canvas bags that had been sewn together so many times only the thread kept them together. We tried to tell him he ruined our well-cultivated image, but he didn't care.

When we got to the golf course is was a beautiful fall day and the greens had just been mowed. "I paid the green keeper to lower the mower," Heart said. "The greens will be so fast spit will roll off of them."

Fast greens and a guy with the yips, this is better than Christmas, I thought.

Montana and his friend were in the bar drinking Bloody Mary's, they knew the right breakfast to have before a big match. Montana was a big man, in his late 40's. He had on expensive golf slacks, white leather golf shoes, and a Polo shirt. His friend was also a big man and looked like a lumberjack. He was wearing ugly plaid short pants with a striped shirt and had on golf shoes that looked like Snead had worn them during his heyday. By his smile I knew it was not going to be an easy match, plus, his short pants matched mine. I ordered a Bloody Mary.

After the drink we headed for the first tee. To my surprise Snake and Freddy were there. Freddy smiled. But I knew why he was there. He was making sure I wasn't going to dump him for part of the action on the other side.

"You don't trust me, Freddy," I said, sounding hurt.

"I don't trust my sister," Freddy said. "And Snake bet on Montana with several other guys. I think he might have set us up."

The match was set. The ball would be played down, every putt had to be holed, $1,000 a man front nine, back nine, and total. The good old nassau bet with a bite.

There is no need to go into all the gory details of the match. Montana could hit the ball as well as anybody I had ever seen. He drove the ball long and hit crisp high irons. But once he was on the green it was as though a demon entered his body. It would take him an eon to putt. He would address the ball

THE GOLF GOD

and wait, and wait, and wait. He would step away from the ball and have to go wipe the sweat from his forehead. Finally, he would take a stab at the putt. But, as golf is, he did stab in one birdie. In golf, like baseball, I see nothing wrong with a guy with the yips getting a designated putter.

Montana's partner was an all around player. They won the first nine by two shots. They shot 32 and we had a 34. Snake loved it. Now you can see how he got his name. Freddy started telling Heart and I what we were doing wrong. Heart asked him, "Do you want to take Buckshot's place?"

Freddy could never beat me unless I played with a blindfold on so he sulked off like a little kid whose Mom had called for him to come home.

As the fortunes of golf go, after seven holes on the back nine, we were three shots up. Which meant, if we held the three shot lead, we would win the back nine and the total and end up winning $1,000 on the day.

Freddy was happy again and trying to figure out a way to not pay me for a few weeks. Bookies have to be good at that sort of thing.

But, they won the 8th hole, and going into the last hole we were only two shots up, meaning if we tied the last hole the match would be a push, and even with my bad math skills I knew it would not pay my rent.

Robert K. Swisher Jr.

What with Montana and the yips it had taken us over six hours to play the match and the sun was now only about fifteen minutes from going down. But, since about the only way to get rid of the yips is to give them to somebody else nobody was going to tell Montana to hurry up.

The last hole is a long par four. It takes a good drive to be able to reach the green with a 3 or 4 iron. The green slopes from the back to the front so bad that if a ball ends up above the hole it is almost impossible to keep the ball on the green with your first putt. To compound an already difficult green there is a swell that runs from the left to the right. A ball on the edge of the swell is an impossible putt. Set in front of the green, about ten yards from the fringe, is a bunker a pirate could bury treasure in and without a map would never find it. A person tries to hit their approach shot barely over the bunker, and either bounce the ball to the front edge of the green or stay short. It is a treacherous hole made even more diabolical by the fact the fairway is tree lined and only 40 yards wide. Most of the time a par will win, very seldom is there a birdie, and a bogey is a good score.

This day the pin was set toward the front of the green where the slope was most drastic, thanks to Heart's green keeper friend - friends in high places always help.

THE GOLF GOD

Montana's partner, hit his tee ball so far left and into the trees it was not even worth looking for. The proverbial, in another zip code shot. "Your hole," he mumbled to Montana.

Montana's drive split the middle.

I could see my rent money going down the drain. My mind was filled with nothing but the vision of a guy with the yips, who had only made one putt all day, canning a 40-foot downhill putt that the Golf God couldn't make. One of those things the Golf God would do. But the Golf God does not have to pay rent. You would think he would be more considerate.

Heart, normally a steady driver, snap hooked his drive into the trees on the left. I took out my 3 wood to play safe, and cut the ball into the trees on the right.

Heart did not say a word as we first found his ball and he played out to the fairway, now a good 5 iron from the hole. I was in fairly decent shape and was able to advance my ball to within an 8 iron away.

Montana's partner's ball was nowhere to be found. And since Snake was Freddy's shadow we knew it was not in Freddy's pocket. Montana, without hesitation, hit a beautiful 4 iron that landed perfectly just over the edge of the bunker, but for some unknown reason, ask the Golf God, the ball did not bite, but bounced and came to rest on the edge of the ridge that ran across the green about ten feet above the hole. The putt was so steep it looked like a ski run only good skiers with a death wish would try.

Heart, old veteran that he was, hit his 5 iron to the front edge of the green. There was no way he could not get down in two. I hit my 8 iron fat and into the bunker. I blasted my next shot about six feet below the hole and marked it.

Heart chipped his shot to within two inches of the cup, walked up and lined up his putt with his wedge and stubbed it, barely moving the ball. I groaned. Freddy had to hold onto a tree to stand up. Heart, still with the wedge, hit the ball in the hole for a six. He looked at Montana as if he didn't have a care in the world and said, "Your putt."

Freddy was now gagging behind the tree.

Montana looked like he had the flu. His face turned ash white and sweat beaded on his forehead. "You can do it," his partner said. "All you have to do is two putt and we win the front and the total."

He had forgotten I still had a putt for bogey. Truthfully, though, a tiny portion of my brain wanted to see Montana make his putt. It wasn't my money, it was Freddy's.

Montana walked below the hole and looked at the putt. He walked to the side of the hole. He

THE GOLF GOD

walked behind his ball. He walked below the hole again. Montana finally addressed the ball, stepped back and took - one, two, three, four, five, six, seven, and on and on and on, practice strokes. He then stopped moving for at least a full minute. He looked like a statue. Another minute passed and still had not moved. It was as though he was frozen in time. It was beginning to grow dark and the sprinkler system on the fairway came on. Montana stepped away from the ball and took several deep breaths and then he looked at me like I was his last friend in the world. He tried to speak, but no words came out. After several more tries he managed to croak, "Buckshot, would you putt?"

Over the protest of Heart I placed my ball down and missed my putt. Heart gave me a dirty look. I shrugged my shoulders. What else would you do with a guy that would putt with a wedge, no matter how short the putt, and for $1,000? Idiot.

Freddy looked at me like I had taken a dive. It is good to keep Freddy confused.

Montana once again walked to the front of the hole. He walked to the side of the hole. The sun was now almost completely down. Montana took his stance and froze - one minute, two minutes, three minutes, five minutes passed. I wondered if we could sell him to a company. They could set his feet in concrete and stick him in the middle of a fountain or they could put a plate on his head and make him into a bird feeder. The outside lights came on at the clubhouse. His partner, walked off the green, got in the cart and drove toward his car. Freddy and Snake, mere shadows, walked away. A few minutes later I heard three cars start up and drive away. Another minute and another, Montana still had not moved.

It was now almost pitch dark and I felt a tap on my arm. I could not make out Heart's face but we walked away like we were passing the casket of an old golf buddy who had just died, one we could normally beat.

Neither of us spoke while Heart drove me home.

The next day at the Fleece Muni not one word was said about the match.

Three days later Freddy came up to me on the driving range and gave me $400. He did not smile. I did not ask any questions.

Montana was never seen again. Any calls to his course were left unreturned. A rumor did float around the following year that he sold his golf course and opened up a bowling alley in Kansas.

The Golf God took a swig of beer, lit a smoke, and with the back of his hand, wiped a tear out of his eye.

CHAPTER TEN
A TRUE GLOSSARY OF GOLF TERMS

"Shanks," the Golf God said. "I am going to tell you what golf terms really mean and I want you to write them down word for word."

I tried, but his words are written down minus the slurring. And, taking poetic license I added one, which I have labeled so not to steal any of the Golf God's glory.

1) Golf: A game of life - mostly filled with misery.
2) Driver: A club that the average golfer should throw away and hit a three wood, but they cost so much now they are mostly carried as a status symbol.
3) 1 iron: Normally carried in the bag so other golfers think you can play the game.

4) Long iron: A club that must be hit after you have messed up your second shot on a par four, or missed two shots on a par five.

5) Fairway wood: What most players hit because a long iron is too hard to hit.

6) Pull: What golfers hit when they want to hook the ball.

7) Push: What golfers hit when there is trouble on the left side of the fairway.

8) Banana Ball: What the majority of golfers hit and call a slight fade.

9) Top: A shot hit under pressure.

10) Shank: There is no definition - ranks almost as high as the yips.

11) Fat shot: Used to plant gladioli bulbs.

12) Scull: A chip shot that goes about 100 yards.

13) Lucky Bastard: Anyone who beats you.

14) Three Jack: Three putting the green. Normally only done when you need a two putt to win.

15) No brainer: A putt that cannot be made. Usually done by your opponent.

16) Gloating: Usually a sign that your game will go to hell after you are ahead a comfortable margin and you end up losing - at which time you are no longer gloating.

17) Stuck: A shot hit so close to the pin even

THE GOLF GOD

Montana could not miss the putt.

18) Hole-in-One: Self explanatory.

19) Par: What you are supposed to get on a hole.

20) Bogey: A par to most people.

21) Double bogey: Excuse time

22) Birdie: One under par on a hole. A normal golfer gets one or two a year.

23) Eagle: When you hole a three wood from 180 yards out on a par five.

24) Green keeper: Somebody who never does anything right and the reason you can never make a putt.

25) O.B.: Hitting one in the parking lot or the cemetery, normally done when all the money is on the line.

26) Bass Ball: A ball hit into a lake, trout ball in the west.

27) Sandy: Getting up and down from a trap.

28) Bump and Run: A shot that is sculled but gets lucky and stops on the green.

30) Yips: When one is unable to putt. Normally a transition in life when the prostate is starting to fail.

31) Hook: What a flat belly can hit.

32) Flat belly: A young player who doesn't know how hard the game is yet.

33) Stick: A good player.

34) Pigeon: What a good player is looking for.

35) Gimme: A putt that is given to you, always one you would have made anyway.

36) Where the Elephants Go to Die: A ball hit so far off line it is not worth looking for. Also what the Roman's called England and Scotland.

37) In Another Zip Code: Same as Where the Elephants go to die excluding the Romans.

38) On the screws: A ball that could not be hit any better. A feeling you have never had.

39) Airmailed: Hitting the ball over the green. Normally the best shot you hit all day.

40) Good Putt: A putt that almost goes in the hole - your opponent will tell you, "good putt."

41) Silence: What you hear from your opponent when you make a good putt.

42) Goof: The real name for golf.

43) Mudder: Playing golf in the rain. Also the first part of a cuss word if you are from the south.

44) Choke: To miss a shot under pressure. Normally a word used by players who are so bad they are never under pressure, so they don't get in the position to choke.

45) Break: The curve of a putt on a green. What you don't play enough of and also what happens to a lot of putters.

46) Divot: For the average player three inches of torn up ground before you hit the golf ball.

47) Look up: Trying to see where the ball is

THE GOLF GOD

going before you hit it. Players who cannot cure this disease should take up bird watching.

48) Caddie: A man who in ancient times carried your golf bag - now called a golf cart.

49) Duffer: A player who plays worse than you do.

50) Women's Day: A day when men learn how to mow the yard.

51) Toe Wedge: A very popular shot and easy to master.

52) Scrambler: A guy who hits the ball all over the golf course and makes a good score. Usually a guy with a good toe wedge game.

53) Handicap: A game where the best liar wins.

54) Good partner: A guy who lies about his handicap.

55) Pro: A man who calls golf work.

56) Fore: A word you yell at the idiots who seem to keep getting in the way of your golf ball in the other fairway.

57) Golfe: How people spelled golf before Mrs. Riley, an English teacher, corrected everybody to the proper spelling, golf.

58) Fairway: Where your ball never goes.

59) Sand Trap: A place that has a rake by it just to look at.

60) Green: A target that is normally missed.

61) Flag or pin: What you hit your putter with

after you miss a putt.

62) Cup or hole: Where the illegal Paganica players hid their feathery.

63) Lip: Where you leave your putt.

64) Slow player: Statement made about a player that has beaten him.

65) Deliberate player: A slow player who is your partner and you are winning.

66) Snap hook: Swinging too hard.

67) Draw: What you did when you were in school.

68) Feather a shot: A term used only by a pro for a high soft cut shot that lands on the green and does not run or back up...lands like a feather...what an average player calls a short, fat, wedge.

69) Lucky: Anybody but you.

70) Good Play: A term used when you win, luck had nothing to do with it.

71) Punch: What you want to do to the guy who beat you.

72) Rough: Where the fairway should be - example - I hit 16 roughs today.

73) Golf Aids: Towels with Vaseline on them, balls with a compression of 145, etc. etc.

74) Golf ball: What you lose only when it is new.

75) Cleat Mark: What your putt hits that made it go in the hole.

THE GOLF GOD

76) Others: A score you made on a hole that was so high even your opponent won't ask you what you got.

77) Smart Golf: I have no idea what this means.

78) Paganica: Rome's only true contribution to the world besides the bikini.

79) Golf Cart: What the modern golfer uses to get around the golf course since our legs have shrunk.

80) Feathery: What the founders of golf called a golf ball because they couldn't say the word, ball.

81) Gutty: The first ball a man could really hit the hell out of. The Top-Flight of its day.

82) Putting God: Probably one of the Golf God's ex-wives. (My addition)

83) Ball Mark Repair Tool: What most golfers leave in their bag.

84) Excuses: What most golfers use instead of blaming themselves. Examples - The green is too fast. The green is too slow. The pin is set too tough. The pin is set too easy. The fairways are too tall. The fairways are too short. The wind is too strong. The people in front of us are too slow. The people behind us are too fast. It's too cold. It's too hot. The greens are too dry. The greens are too wet. The tree was in the way. The rough is too tall. There is not enough rough. The bunker is too deep .... etc ...etc ...etc ...etc ..." Try and remember two things," the

Golf God said. "What is fair for one is fair for all, and, there are no excuses."

CHAPTER ELEVEN
THE GOLF GOD'S 14 RULES

"Shanks, do you really know the one thing that really peeves me off about modern golf?" the Golf God asked.

"Not enough beer carts on the course," I said.

"Not funny," the Golf God said, opening another beer.

"Truthfully, I wouldn't have the faintest idea," I said.

"There are too many rules," he exploded angrily, his face turning red and his eyes bulging.

It's not nice seeing a God about to have a coronary.

The Golf God composed himself, lit a smoke, and took several deep drags. "When golf started there was only one rule," the Golf God said calmly. "After a golfer teed off he never got to touch the ball unless it was in a pile of bones."

"Where did the bones come from?" I asked.

"Englishmen, Scotsmen, and a few sheep."

I didn't have a chance to comment when the Golf God continued. "Now there are so many rules to the game it takes a golf cart to haul the rulebook around."

"Man has a tendency to muck up anything that is simple," I said.

"Why is that?" the Golf God asked seriously.

"You are supposed to have the answers," I said.

"Being a God is more confusing than you think," he said.

I really didn't know how to reply to a Golf God who was having a slight bummer.

"Ok, write these down," the Golf God said. "These are my 14 rules of golf and notice I call these rules, not commandments."

******

1) Do not talk while a competitor hits or putts. If you like to talk all the time become a radio announcer.

2) Do not laugh out loud when an opponent hits one out-of-bounds, into the trees, bunker, pond, or other trouble. You may snicker under your breath.

THE GOLF GOD

3) Do not stomp an opponent's path of his ball on the green, either by accident or on purpose. This is a grievous no no and will result in serious retribution from the Golf God.

4) Rake the damn sand traps.

5) Do not call an opponent who is cheating any bad names. Any golfer who tells me he has not cheated is not on his way to golf heaven.

6) Do not gloat in any way that can be seen. Gloat with a sympathetic look on your face.

7) Help your opponent look for a lost ball. You do not have to look where you think the ball might be, but you should go through the motions.

8) Rake the damn sand traps.

9) Never, never, count your money before the match is over.

10) Replace your divots. There are a few lost souls who still cling to the purest view and play the ball down. Give the poor dying breed a break.

11) Fix your ball mark on the green. That is if you hit a green. Chip marks do not count.

12) Pay your losses with a smile and then go home and yell at your spouse. The Golf God is very understanding how a spouse can get in the way of a good game of golf.

13) Rake the sand traps you lazy jerks.

14) On the golf course conduct yourself like the government.

"That's it," the Golf God said.

"That's it?" I said, feeling like I had missed something.

"Shanks, if I made it too complicated you golfers would get confused."

"What do you mean by conduct yourself like the government?" I asked.

"You have to figure that one out," he said.

"You mean on the course we should look like we really care what other people do when in fact we only care about ourselves," I said.

"That's good, Shanks, you can do anything you want as long as you keep saying it's for the good of the people."

"What is the one man made rule of golf that riles you the most?" I asked.

"Two shots for a lost ball. Go figure. What is wrong with one penalty stroke?"

"I don't know."

"An out- of- bounds is two shots, a lost ball is two shots, but a ball in the water is only one shot. It doesn't make any sense. A ball in the water is also lost. Every penalty should be one shot. It would simplify matters."

"That makes sense to me," I said. I get enough penalties anywhere I could shave a shot would help.

"I can tell you one thing that is not nice but you

THE GOLF GOD

will never get any grief from me when you do it," the Golf God said. "When a car drives by a golf course and you and your friends are playing and people in the car holler "fore" it is proper for golfers to make nasty gestures at the car. Anybody who would stop their car and run over to four men with clubs in their hands has to be a fool."

"It's strange what people do," I said.

"It is strange. People don't drive by tennis courts and holler "volley." They don't drive by swimming pools and holler "splash." They don't drive by bowling alleys and holler "gutter ball.""

I felt the Golf God was getting a little carried away so I cut in. "You know Golf God, you are not handsome, you dress like a bum, you drink and smoke too much, and more times than not you are not fair to a person while they play, but you like your followers, I know you do."

I could see both happiness and sadness in the Golf God's eyes. "I love you all," he said softly. "You are the only reason I am."

CHAPTER TWELVE
WHY WE PLAY GOLF

"I want you to do me a favor," the Golf God said.

"You want another beer."

"No. I want you to tell me in your own words why people play golf.

"It would be my pleasure," I said – surprised that the Golf God would respect my opinion.

The Golf God relaxed in the chair, crossed his hands over his belly, rested his head back, and shut his eyes.

"When it comes down to it, Golf God, it is very simple, golfers are dreamers, we embrace hope and never give up on the dream," I said.

The Golf God opened his eyes and smiled. "You are a good disciple, Shanks," he said.

"Thank you," I replied.

We sat in silence for a long time. The Golf God contentedly sipping on a beer and seemingly

THE GOLF GOD

relaxed. I went to the bathroom. When I came back the Golf God was not in my chair. I figured he was in the kitchen getting another beer. But after a few minutes, and not hearing any noise, I looked in the kitchen and then all over the house. He was gone. I quickly looked outside to see if he had stolen my car, but my car was still in the driveway.

I was about to sit in my chair when I saw a letter with a twenty-dollar bill on top of it in the seat of the chair. This is the letter.

"Shanks, I hope all you golfers at least once can a downhill putt on a green that is as fast as ice. I hope you sail an iron over a lake and the ball lands close to the hole. I hope you blast the ball out of a trap and the ball ends up so close to the hole it is a tap in. I hope you get a hole in one. I hope you scull shots, hit the ball out of bounds, top the ball, shank it, and have days you can't hit the side of a barn. I hope you five putt at least once. It's all golf, it's all part of the game, enjoy it while you can. Hit the ball and chase it, hit it and chase it, good old Paganica, it all ends up the same anyway. I enjoyed my visit. The next time I come I will give you more advice about golf and you can tell me more of your stories. And Shanks, keep your head still when you putt, your flinching."

Robert K. Swisher Jr.

******

I have never seen the Golf God again, but I have felt his presence when a man who has never shot less than 100 is strutting proudly around the clubhouse showing people his scorecard with the 99 circled in red. I have felt him while lining up a putt and knowing the ball was going in the hole. I have also heard him laugh when I have slashed the ball deep into the trees. I look forward to the Golf God's next visit. If you see him before I do send him my way, and tell him twenty bucks did not cover the pizza and beer tab. But it doesn't matter - being with him was worth the money. Also tell him I am making a lot of putts and I hope he is not in too much trouble with his ex-wife for giving me a putting tip.

THE END

TO EXPLORE MORE OF ROBERT K. SWISHER JR'S NOVELS VISIT:

http://www.swisherbooks.com/

www.ingramcontent.com/pod-product-compliance
Lightning Source LLC
Chambersburg PA
CBHW050439010526
44118CB00013B/1603